THE BACK CHANNELS

THE BACK CHANNELS

JENNIFER HOULE

Clarise Foster, Editor

Cover design by Doowah Design.
Photo of Jennifer Houle by October Afternoon Photography.

This book was printed on Ancient Forest Friendly paper.
Printed and bound in Canada by Hignell Book Printing Inc.

We acknowledge the support of The Canada Council for the Arts and the Manitoba Arts Council for our publishing program.

Library and Archives Canada Cataloguing in Publication

Houle, Jennifer, 1977–, author
The back channels / Jennifer Houle.

Poems.
ISBN 978-1-927426-84-5 (paperback)

I. Title.

PS8615.O8498B33 2016 C811'.6 C2016-901628-5

Signature Editions
P.O. Box 206, RPO Corydon, Winnipeg, Manitoba, R3M 3S7
www.signature-editions.com

For my mom, my dad and my sister
& for Tyler and the boys

Contents

SHEDIAC, NEW BRUNSWICK

CROSSWALK

Tongues

In estuarine waters
tongues of intertidal mud
quarrel and thrust. Fuming
bedmates wrestle, interlocked,
tussle out of Shepody,
war at every confluence,
lash over deltas and flats.

≈

Salmon, gaspereau and smelt,
replaced by *Sentinelles,* haunt
the silt, phosphorescent
bones blazing through sediment,
hammering the sluiceway,
exiled, Acadian ghosts
boring into the headpond.

≈

We meet where tributaries
peter out. The arguments
end abruptly. Clogged, stunted.
There's nowhere else. We turn back,
follow freshets ferrying
winterkill through dirty grooves
in chastened, lukewarm runnels.

≈

Thick splits in the freezing muck
mesmerize the swollen gulls
fed by the mall's parking lot,
perched on mangled shopping carts
hurled down cracked embankments,
scavenging the riverside,
watchful eyes stalking the slits.

♒

X marks us. One day we will
have this neighbourhood thing down:
the bleached and fretted bark chips,
maples gored like soldiers brained
with 50-cals, the poplars
maimed, but philosophical,
leaning in close as they can.

THE BACK CHANNELS

Talk of Mermaids

This is the shift of the heart's tumbled pin,
the bloodshot eye and the haul: smokers trickle
from the old *boucanerie*, converted now,
one body, one bad lung, a rotting arctic char

between them: web of sick, soft tissues. Nets
of spittle, wry grins, unenviable shrewdness.
Banned crab heaved into slatted wirebounds
leaks into cynical chat. Dreaded things

are sure now, handed down, and trawling
for a private place to die, they ring our darkest
impulses and vex small acts of kindness
with a nervous calculation, shy self-interest.

Now is not the time for talk of mermaids,
questionable motives, far-fetched sentience,
or the pain of others. Skepticism rears
its double, whiskered chin, disarticulating

wonder with a grunt. Heavy snowfall
is predicted, work is to be done. Everywhere
we look, stock images: a hull shears cold,
black water in dead silence. Nothing floats,

nor swims, to the surface. Only when you turn
your back, a fin on the horizon. Excitations
kin to the aurora borealis fumble and fail
beautifully, trying something different.

First Trimester

I'm sure you're fine. The body is a rough draft,
full of qualms and broken lines. Murky,
secretive, a muddle of mixed metaphors
all wanting at the heart. Though it insists
on its intent, on being what it is and things
being what they are. You have to laugh.

I don't mean your body. I mean mine.
I am here now, having begged a little nap,
to settle, to imagine settling perfectly
in a quiet, swaddled hour. I can hear
your brother's tinny ruckus in the kitchen,
and your father's added ruckus. Peace

is nonsense. I have come to worry
in warm, soft, synthetic down. For what
it's worth, to worry at the nib of you,
the tendril and the thought. And if the body
is the road to hell. And if it's not.
And just what is beyond control?

My thoughts. They've settled on a course,
as you have settled on a course – Aurora? Finn?
Not to be frightened or full of irrational guilt.
If the twist came, always, from within,
from pure intent. If something didn't, always,
have to act upon our will to change our ways.

The Past

The past is uncontrollable.
It's at the back door with a knife.
It's at the front door with a deep red
flash drive in the shape of genitalia.

It is everywhere and nowhere
like your very particular ghosts.
It is all you've ever known of love.
Every day, it beats you home, drifts
into the house through the vents.

It turns on your computer.
You know the cadence of its lament.
You can't stop it, though you've heard.

It gathers and accumulates
like snow in the worst winters,
on the roof and in the gutters.
Makes it so you cannot see
what's coming around corners.

Piles up. Dreams and details
enter its mouth like krill and algae
into a whale. What it swallows,
it becomes, irrevocably, as we
become what we ingest, time

and time again. It can't be looked at,
not in the face. We glean as much
as we can. It is almost all there is.
It is our only source of light.

Gathering

T'aimais ma blouse violette. Ben, c'était pas vraiment une blouse—I don't know the word for what it was—stretchy material, ridged, a button-up, in style at the time. Gathering, pre-clubs, sur un de tes chums. *Un gaddaring,* I mocked. Moi, j'voulais pas être là j'étais gênée, j'me sentais out of place avec le monde de Cap-Pelé, j'me sentais mal a l'aise. *Come on,* t'as dis, *ya personne qui va te mordre, pi j'aimerais right ça que tout le monde te mitte. Je te brag tout le temps.* Ej voulais pas que tu saves about ma hell adolescence, pi je voulais right pas être la loser chick, pas back. The way those French girls stare at you, like valley girls from bad films circa 1983, but even more matérialiste. *It's fucking patented,* I told you, said I couldn't take those awful girls. Cast me out, when we were kids, stood back and watched me take the brunt from wounded sons I didn't know enough to know were hurting at the time. In later years, some of them apologized. But pas les filles, ah man—eux-autres enjoyed it, I suspect. Not that those specific girls were there, no, they were off at university in Ottawa, Quebec et en Paris. But there I was, under the trees, smoking Du Mauriers, picking at the grass, noting constellations, watching you shake hands, knock fists, beer after beer was slapped into your palm, your shoulder punched, in contrast to my bitterness, my stultifying grudge. Listening to the girls radotte—I guess I should admit I thought them dumb, and wasn't very nice myself. I thought them one-dimensional: hockey boys and hockey hair, wedding plans and pictures of their dogs. *On va shopper pour des robes à la weekend. J'aime right out le truck a ton boyfriend, c'est ti un standard? Hey, comment longtemps que ça fait que vous êtes ensemble, cause moi je croyais— Ah vrai ? Right on.* I said I was the first person you called when you came home from out West and one girl looked about to lose her shit. She sank her drink. You didn't leave me by myself for very long. Pulled me back between the boat and the garage and said again *violette te fais.* I didn't want to ask *faut-il qu'on reste?* but pinned your wrists to that girl's lawyer dad's brick wall.

The Point

loosely after Edwin Morgan's translation of Eugenio Montale's "Lindau"

Sleek with mist, the gull,
with sea moss in his beak,
returns to the yellow buoy.

Night falls on the wharf again.
Turgid water laps the gravel
and cement blocks, painting
them with a film of diesel.

Over and over, thoughtlessly,
blinking neon beer signs
father short-lived shadows
that go tumbling down
the greasy banks.

At Captain Dan's,
the drunk women weave
from deck to bar, knocking
back purple shot after
shot, up on the tables
and chipped green benches,

unaware of the discordant bass
pounding into their summer hit
from the nearby throng
of idling speedboats.

School

I left the classroom humming "Teenage Frankenstein"
and hit the bleachers. Didn't give a good goddamn about
the starving children we'd been fed all afternoon.
A woman has to prove that she is viable with talk,

but I had done with masquerading and hoped Julie would go die.
A crucial player took it in the knees. The clock ran out, blinked
dumbly down on us. And who'd believe I didn't turn around,
but crossed the field, a lady, nibbling a knuckle, dainty—

dainty as my fingernails the night he guessed my nipples
would be pale and I refused to prove him wrong.
A massive sound was building in my chest, amplified,
distorted, set to hurl me through a windshield if my heart

could not keep up. A camel-toe, a bitch slap, a banana comb
in shards: a tortoiseshell mosaic on the pave behind the school.
This cannot be my life, is what I said, and no one moved.
Transatlantic winds carried the smoky, toadstool breath of fallen

leaves, rain gutters, and mud into my lungs. I couldn't breathe.
Forever stopped to slug me on the arm, and blew the scene.
The clock reset, my dress torn at the seams. Nobody believed
a dome would rise: palladium of furtive, first exchange.

Sly finger-palm trysts between the seats were never meant
as prostitution. Still, they gave me names. I was the world.
Weren't we all? A massive sound contracted and expired
in my chest. Learning institutions glowered in the mist.

Acadie Noir

We want to know about the oldest house.
And how to screw the storied tragedy
we've toddled from, yet hitch ourselves

to it wholly, paint it on with a star
and flaunt survival, flaunt the beer garden,
broken French, slurred, glad heart

of the village in summer, broke for the fun
of it, broken irreverently, broken as we saw fit.
We want lanterns and bug lights, repellant in pails

to ward off the will o'the wisps, frolicking glints
in the shapeshifting dark of the deep, gaseous swamps
of our childhood nightmares, where movie stars waltzed

through sad, clapboard houses, old lace yawning
into the windless night air. We want cars that will start
and sober relations, parents who know when to turn

on the lights, and who will tell us straight about
all the old houses, the solitudes hitching on over oceans
in bottles and tubs, and the whips and the lashes,

crimes running like shine down splintering staircases.
Bury the cross and the guilt of our mothers
and we will serve shellfish with pride in brochures.

Give us bonfires and lanterns and good car insurance
and we will restore widows' peaks and wainscoting,
let will o' the wisps even dare with our husbands.

The Back Channels

There was talk of building a cathedral once,
then a bistro — jewel of a boardwalk that would sluice
along the pulpy banks where many streams ran
parallel, and sometimes pooled, argued and frothed
amongst each other before diverging, altered
by the tussle. Their activity was monitored.

What, we had to know, was being fostered
in those creeks? Our listening devices settled
in the still, deep vaults of beaver dams. But it
was hard to know. There is what water does
to sound. There were codes we couldn't crack.
The call of a loon often interfered, jammed

our systems with noise. Gulls and peepers
hid their eggs in our machines, and much
was lost in the mess of births. One night,
an awful flapping of wings struck us dumb.
The steady burble we had been a long year
sequencing did not resume. Intermittent

wails of mourning pierced the unfamiliar roil.
The only constant was the rotten tang of mink.
An aerie disappeared. We watched the logjams
as they happened, and resolved themselves.
We realized it would never profit us to build.
We found no reason to continue listening in.

Crops

Another day of bird shit on the produce,
wilted kale. *Brassica oleracea,* broccoli
like disease. First light of the mean time,
crow piss, annelid's retreat. What we can
begin anew, we will begin anew,
reluctantly, on the cheap. State of mind
like bait's opposing angel, you turn
scarecrow in the corn-maze in the middle
of peak season. Tourism is dead,
is death, turned on us. Business
slow, we slouch like helpless,
strong-armed elms along the pitted
old road to the tavern. Any orchard
in a blight, before the harvest.

Service Roads

Kind of a story where old men, toothless,
on their bicycles will stop, kick up
a suffocating cloud of aggregate and rust
to warn you off. Old, or otherwise
auxiliary, offbeat characters churned

from the centre. Frowsy, boxy, dimwitted
redheads, aging protestors and hags
willing the bulrushes to cackle. Maybe
the warning alone is the crux. To have
come this far and seen so much and find

you still can laugh it off, dismiss it all
easily as religion—more easily still
than what you wanted to believe: Bigfoot
tracks in the pit party woods out back
of the busted trestle, where you met

with your badass lot every last Saturday
all summer, riding out shotgun with Timmy
and Ferg, and after a brutal night in the bars
to have finally stumbled on charred remains
in the trampled yard of a backwoods lean-to

stacked to the rafters with arcane books: proof
of old cults and shit in the fields, only to find
it gone the next weekend, if you ever did
manage: so many equidistant dirt roads
running into transposable thickets. Always,

you twig on one birch or stone, and yeah —
this could be the way we came that afternoon.
You almost want to meet a drifter off his nut
with visions of doom, cracking warnings good
for a chuckle, and stories to hook your new girl.

Weak Force

Notes from the Global Reservation Centre
Moncton, Night Shift, 2005

1.

We'll need dedicated lines to lodge complaints.
Our ice cream melted. The emperor bit me.

One guy told me the trees were our future.
Trees. But for now, the hope is bacteria.
Grown in labs, made to eat up the oil slicks.
Last week a sick duck coughed up an alien.

Listen, that blonde woman interfered with me,
wrote-up my sandals, my big toe un-businesslike.
Better for her if she doesn't talk to me.

2.

So weird: a moose barged into
the Cornwall Point Wilsons, antlers
nosing the local paper, a day too early
to see himself in there. Somehow,
he made it half a kilometer. One woman
ran, dropped her lottery ticket.

Miracle? Omen? Cannot imagine.
Late for my shift, though, on account of it.
Wildlife, I told them. I might not make it.
Monarch butterfly in my driveway.
Flapped its gorgeous, endangered wing.
So screw ya. No, go screw yourself
then. Here's the thing.

3.

Over lunch, on 9/15
I told an absolutist,
a prognosticating woman:
it'll be okay.

Oh please, she spat, and I was sad for her.
Of course, I'd been

expecting something, felt the upsurge,
history lurching, that whole summer
I dreamt of towers, teenagers
stealing my keys and lovers.

September 6th: And in this dream, I bombed
a lookout, wondered where to head for, after.
End of an ending, endless era —

What doesn't fall in autumn weather?

That was it for introspection. My hand,
near hers, was of little comfort.

I would have been 23. Was,
actually, and sweet, offered my hand,
agreed to drinks, shared my cigarettes,
answered the phone. Attracted the grief-
stricken, over and over. Nodded, concurred,
said I am so sorry. God, but I wasn't, though.

Nothing could make me.

4.

Then how doggedly it meandered.
Instinctively found its way to town,
drawn by porch light and the conversation
we'd been having all those years.

How it climbed over dusty backhoes,
and threaded its way through pitchforks,
and spun its web between the rusted
husks of mufflers. How it bedded down
in green refrigerators, one after the next,
and left itself no breadcrumb trail,
no way of getting home.

Television in October

I can't keep looking: the colors are mad,
the story too simple, a crude exaggeration
of the news. I used to watch religiously.

I was young and could stand, could even
wish for vampirism, fused, re-polarized
shadows, merging and changing. I could lie

awake all night marking changes. Entering
each transition with a hook, getting what I needed.
I still want the picturesque, the soft, familiar

and sublime at once, but not like this. I want little
aspen leaves on red-mud roads. No suggestion
of untimely death. Just a lovelier way home,

through beautiful, appropriate decay, where what
bursts its vesicle is gold, triumphant, recomposes
what culminates. Where the road runs off the page,

keeps up its tones, leads everywhere, and everywhere
is only one small town, inhabited, beloved, devoid
of duplicitous storefronts. Where there is nothing

to show, nothing dark to elucidate, where falling leaves
are not ambiguous and it will be forever fall, a gorgeous,
timely plunge. I have sickened of this light, this mean

fluorescence exposing all wounds, entering us with a swab
and suspicions, and already knowing what we'll find:
again and again: the body is hauled up out of the river.

Who still can stomach the demands of narrative?
The camera pans away – there are so many trees,
it's dark. We're left again with what remains, under
the hushed luminance of earthlight and the moon.

Representative

Last night, I went to Costco for a shirt I'd seen
last weekend, stocking up on frozen food,
and the sunset from Foch's Bridge on my way home,
made me ugh — breeze off the bay was vinegar.

Motorhomes obscured the drainage mottled shore,
gulls and paper lanterns drooped, antenna sagged,
inverted sails bisected the horizon. I needed
a new shirt for work after a week of feeling plain.

My skirts are all knee-length. How do you do you
ever show initiative? I know I am supposed
to project confidence, but so much shit goes down
just getting crab flaked, I refuse to smile until

they really put the screws to me and twist.
You put your ear to carcass and you'll hear
the coast complaining like it does. Close
your eyes in sunlight, you'll see flags.

Open them in sunlight: idiot. Close your eyes
in sunlight, close your eyes, you'll hear the protestors
retreat the way they came, blustering, the whoosh
of some bad settlement is always in the wind.

Bois-Joli

I don't listen much for birds. They won't tell me where
you've gone, which city you are in, what kind of work.
I have finished with the vigil in the forest, given up

on wilderness, on taking the word of indigenous
plants. Queen Anne's, stitchwort, goatsbeard
and tickseed flower into bristled obsolescence.

I don't hack the splintered deadfall into slats slapped
with your visage, or etch your name into weathered
placards I might nail to the milliard junctures

I have designated at random. I won't candy violets
or make a tea of red clover. Broom and hay give
over to muck that resonates with me now.

It is always wet. All quag and evil stepmothers
sashaying queenly into the clearcuts, wise to the ruse
of deer heart. Or I pretend them in the fog, willing

myself to remain a princess. Fruitlessly. Old wild apple
trees snarled in birch give over to larch swale hemmed
by logging roads narrow as crows' throats. Every shaft

of nauseating light falls on wordless living matter
coaxed into doomed travails. Movement is a slow wind
through a brown field into a deceptive dun expanse

there is no rediscovering. Way does not lead on to way
so much. I circle, circle. It is easy to get home, though
home is drifting. Tractors rust in stubby alder copses.

I watch disease spread, wonder what stunts.
It doesn't matter where I'd like to go or what I used
to toy with building: toolsheds, benches. You've been gone

so long I could be anyone, and everything is foliage:
a gutwrench of dapple adorning dead ends. You're not
among the pollen cones fallen into the litter, you were not

stolen by fern ring sprites. I don't look for red cloth snagged
on severed branches, nor am I hunting a place of worship:
the lodge I'd have come upon, nailed shut, secluded.

Old Shediac Road

No one's gonna know what really happened on that job.
Bottom line is now: lifelong bad back.

Bit of dried blood on the Cat's dinged, yellow haunch,
camouflaged by mud and shredded wrack.

Could be a small animal's, spatter of coyote's kill,
or someone trying to escape from Shediac,

hitcher on the old road, thumbing out,
EI claim denied, on his last pack.

Four wheels stuck in mud, council entrenched.
Planning commission sniffs—mean, shitty hacks

intent on water mains and new hotels,
contractors turning tricks behind the haystacks.

Rue Beaubassin

Split-entry, *la plupart.*
Totally pedestrian and full
of squalid basement rooms,
painted in daycare blues. The porches off
of the side-doors lean and go *pas*
mal pitched to cracked pave walks,
louche with cress and sickly buttercups
and close-knit bugleweeds — and you

are the same old meddling spy, ever
the runt of the neighbourhood's
seedtime, squatting to peer
with an ordered loop

into the pilled, clay ant castles
(rivaling) flanking the stoop.

Urban Development Poles

Now this word — poles. Distracting. I know
what happens with poles. What's lost in the division
stays lost, eh? Thing about poles — you can't
have three, but I defy you not to contemplate

the poly-polar landscape's sad tryst with urbanity.
Who doesn't love a dirty, multi-focal love?
Still. What happens in Moncton, stays. Gets
a shitty place off Elmwood and starts applying

for jobs. Once, I tried to leave and Calgary spat
me back, a wayward fishbone. My grandmother
warned me I'd be raped, but she was wrong.
And I was never anybody's waitress, for that matter.

*

So, what brings you home? An overdue apology,
le littoral, a death? I knew it was time when some
guy started calling on my cell, asking for Mathieu.
And I don't know any Mathieu—well, I knew twelve.

Then I started dreaming about Shediac deformed —
where Main Street was, I put a potato farm. Twitched:
a stand of pine. A pharmacy. A pet store. *Witch*, a spectral
biker hissed. I raised my finger to the moon (a Shell sign

I mistook) and blinked again. Cultural Imports. Please
Apply Within hung on the door. Now this word:
tolls. I'm strung along, gliding the sinuous colonnade
of posts along the transport corridor. Back and forth —

what's gained in the exchange? The thoroughfare becomes
the fling that shifts the poles at home. What's been
misplaced turns up when you begin to pack your things.
What's lost washes ashore, bloated, after the sea change.

STAGHORN

Brilliance

This isn't rocket science, this
nursing the rocket scientists
until my nipples have bleared
into the shapes of unnamed,

endangered wetlands, denuded,
abraded. I have only to give
a reason for the waves
of shadows, only to say what

a shadow is, every evening
a different phantom, what it knows,
what it eats and doesn't eat,
where it goes. I have only to

kiss the soft soles of their feet
and count their fingertips, each
and every, name the whorls
of their baby thumbs. It is so

physically easy to love.
I don't need another degree.
I don't need my old fierce beauty.
I have only to drive the car,

only to narrate the scene.
Little monkey, that is a star.
That was a vivid dream.
Only to know what it means.

Staghorn

Nobody I asked could say what you were called.
Omnipresent bit of shrub, hedge plant, running
with your ruby drupes, between old properties.

Spinner to your Rumpelstiltskin, I dug up your handle,
dredged for it, searched for red, conical fruit, velvety
russet flowers, common ornamental. Finally,

I learned you are indigenous and useful, wont to
make a healing lemonade or tea, that you're a mordant,
of all things, cause what's a mordant? Substance

that helps dye to set, to really stain the toughest cloth.
Your berries can be smoked. Beekeepers burn your pods.
Though I have yet to meet someone who paid you any

mind or knew they saw you, every day. Knew you
were growing in their own yards, or fretting the fence
half the length of their favourite walk, interspersed

with alder and wild roses, all along the riverbank, root
systems spreading inland. It's difficult to fathom you,
to make sense of the symmetry: your shapely, stony fruit

well-kept and orderly. Then you are a tangle of soft antlers,
thickset branches curling into Celtic knots. Having spawned
long lines of cultivars, you are an original, an icon,

where it all began. Spiraling through centuries, anonymous,
you blend unseen into our gardens, throw your snarled shade
onto walkways and promenades, lending curb appeal,

serving your strange purposes, performing your odd tasks,
and persevering, almost unremarked, mother and father, both,
at times, keeper of yourself, offshoots all unstudied and unsung.

Blueberries

All stain, no sting: defenseless, quick to rot,
crushed into the summer nightmares of the boneless,
muted bodies hemmed amorphous in skin thin
and purpling with a sex that sings to voles,
maggots, aphids, nutritionists.

Mummy berries clinging to the vine,
clusters of distended husks conjuring dodder,
arthropods and earthbound spirits lurking in sod and twig.

Not To Be Confused

For my grandmother, Sheila

Palliative. Not to be confused with *palliare*, to cloak, although
the mauves and greens, the rooftop patio with pleasance, and the paper

white geraniums were a blanket of hushed tones, as were the nurses'
voices, muted flannelettes in the communal lounge, insipid jokes

we told each other and told you, the highlight reels we pulled
out of our asses. Oh. You never cared for that kind of language,

and the truth is we spoke French all afternoon, distancing with
loanwords: *infarctus massive, accident vasculaire, nécrose,*

imprévu. All Greek to you. I'm ready to go home.
In the eleventh hour, you expired, clever, and the television

crackled, went to snow, a sharp concurrence which meant
everything to some, though others scoffed. I was restrained.

I held your small, bruised hand and thought *lâche pas*
and I did not want to let go. The television sparked, and cawed,

and sputtered, went to snow. I heard my mother fall.
She hated crows. You taught me stars and the words shepherd, once,

upon. I knelt and said aloud the only prayer I know, the same one
that, unbidden, I self-soothe with, even now, not to be confused

with counting stars or irises, or the toast and tea you ordered,
churlish, miffed, astoundingly awake, and lucid, in your thirst.

Lemons

Life gives you lemons and you make a centerpiece.
Bowlfuls, trailing borage, sprigged with mint.

Lead crystal flutes refract the lemon-light
into a changeable arrangement

of disoriented motes, feebly ascending
into water-stained crown mouldings

through parched mouths in blistered paint.

As if light cleaning were a summer
afternoon ballet, impromptu, triggered by the slant

adagio of thoughtful presentation, a final blue-
starred vine of cure for inflammation, wedged:

iced cucumber soothing in effect, a cultivated
slicer to tired skin and swollen lids.

Ring Box

October is so pitiless, the baby squirrels kazoo
distress from maples holding out against gold,
red senescence. The outer edges are first
to turn. Many of the leaves fall with their hearts

still green as May. This is like my excess.
Take this ring box I'm getting rid of.
It houses a screw-you letter never sent,
begotten by convictions that, though moth-eaten,

still rile me to choose. I recall their evolution
and could give you ballpark figures—what I lost:
a Dodge, a mattress, careful notes, a bronze Ganesha,
pennants, Nanny's quilt. Look: this painting

I will sell you for ten bucks, this book
I'll never read again, like new. Concerns humble
beginnings and great loss, but not much of a page-turner.
It's like you just stop caring, halfway through.

Staying

Something wicked nests in
the meninges that encapsulate
routine, pistol butted hard
against the nape of habit's neck.

Hornets off the porch.
I knock back lemon fizz and eye
the swarm, feet dangling off the side
into snarled cowslip and plantain sedge,
calves twitching dissent after a day spent
raking rills in storebought dirt.

There is anxiety in the water.
And there is something in my drink.
All that effervescence, placated.

My cup's half full of muted sunset,
a clouded, gritty mix.

Whatever it is I'm feeling.
Flies perch on the lip.

Pteridology

In my living room, a struggling
fern dreams of a yellow spore,
juts from its silvered pot in a condemning
disarray of green and russet foliage,
black spores drilling through indusium,
shedding wizened fingers onto the planed,
wooden back of an imported elephant: tusk up.

Nothing you can do will save a fern this lost.
Leaves splayed from one another for survival,
or in accusation, have gone corporate woman mad
competing with themselves for every mineral,
each swig. A new position, fresh nutrient sticks,
but hard to say. The wrong light for so long,
electric heat and city water — what might it take

for a love spell plant plunked into a discount
alloy maw to recreate itself, sprout even one
last elongated frond, comforting and baffling me
with patterns, until shamed, if reassured,
I promise its next born children pergolas?

Late Lunch

Even the half hour is pressed for time.
A seven minute string of glaring lies,
a battle of strategic bites and digs and prods
devised to fence each other into revelations
that could not survive the short and brutal afternoon.

A twenty minute stalemate, then we split the bill,
divest ourselves by reading takeout menus
for the harried ninety seconds we won't fill.

Night does fall early now. A gross multeity
of intersecting routes presages traffic
we're already caught in. It is sadly à propos
to say sleep tight instead of have a good one,
over-tired as we are, and heavy-lidded, knowing
we'll be kept awake till dawn with indigestion.

Paid Parking

You feel it in your palms when things get by you.
Short-lived squalls displace a pile of desiccated oak leaves

blown in all the way from Maine. A towering casino
could revitalize these blocks, recast debris as opulent,

aggressive, overdue. The ball is dropping, always,
in this undeveloped space. Low down flows of feces,

rust, and wrappers travel under foot traffic, move in
and out of temporary homes stacked five on five,

bridging into pyramid on one another's backs: the lonely
acrobalance of contracting in close quarters in a city

tired of sucking in its gut. Here is just the danger
of a wasp sting, busked harmonica's screed please,

and there's your doppelganger, honey, doing windmills
on his in-line skates. *Kerang* of a tipped barrel, out of eyeshot,

interrupts the rolling thrum of carts, collected bottles, double
strollers, and the ordinary prattle of bandy-legged moms

in cut-off jeans, tarred flips gumming asphalt to the mail,
sweat ivied to their necks in transient tattoos. Really,

I just park here now, my parking paid by work, a minor coup,
the first of many minor coups, and victories unsung

by VLT's ka-ching. I've been saved sixty bucks a month,
and this is good, demanding something more like what

you're worth, the biggest risk of all. No need to be
careful what we do here, people's lives are portable,

fit snugly in their phones, and leases, everybody knows this,
can be broken. You cross that bridge when its time.

Medium Beige

On the built-in, speckled vanity
lie implements of tedium. A flat-iron,
tacky with the residue of product
from this morning, tourmaline plates
waiting in their wire heap to pull
my matted waves into respectability,
with a little help from argan oil,
which is only lately *de rigueur*.

And other various pomades and fixatifs.
I remember paying thirty dollars, once,
to have my hair glossed. I was in first year,
a wreck in Halifax, but I had the shiniest hair
on Robie Street. I always held it up to the sun,
then let it fall—a slow flip. All the way home
on the train, that year, I let the play of gold
and violet pigments occupy me, thankful
for the light that came in at the window.

My shade now derives, in part, from lavender,
though it is nearly black. Sometimes, the dye
is not available: ingredients still growing.
Everything organic, sulfate-free. Loose
mineral powder, stiff kabuki brush
and subtle blush in coffee rose fit nicely
in a Tupperware container in the vanity's
top drawer. The bluish plastic bothers me,
of course, but nothing else has worked.
The hemp and sisal bags and the woven
baskets all leached powder and pencil
shavings, smirching the white laminate.

Nestled there as well is my gold-plated
eyelash curler, like the hand-worked jaw
of a baby croc, freckled with mascara.

This device, I used to think, was glamorous.
Babysitters had them. Liz and Amy used them.
Far as I can tell, it makes no difference.
My eyes appear to be no more open.

I've gleaned what I could from magazines,
but no one ever really showed me how to part
and elongate my lashes—not even when we used
to make each other up, lining each other's lids,
our breath on each other's faces. One night,
Lizzie gave me one eye whore, one innocent.
I was trying not to study her too much
as she applied the kohl and silver, so I missed
the art of what she'd done. It's too late now:
most acquire the knack in young adulthood
or abandon the pursuit.

I am afraid to. Next to the sink,
a soapstone Aphrodite, dusted with a film
of luminizing bronzer, oversees the plucking,
remnant of the time when I believed that there
was something sacred in the daily undertaking.
I know it now to be mundane. The goddess I gaze on
is factory-made. We will not be starting any wars.
Prettiness relies upon an aggregate, an average.
And the prettiest are clung to. So I spend
the hour it takes to generate a face, completely
unobjectionable, warm medium beige.

Bad Movies

Avarice was going to be civilized and silver; hell, the rustic haunts
of monstrous adolescents: tire swings, car lots and empty lodges ranged
in crude half-circles like small handfuls of thrown bones, a demimonde

of lakes and absent parents, trembling aspens going bottle-blonde,
rail thin, ashen, shaking out a wraithlike prettiness — impossible fixation.
There was a particular aesthetic. Steely noir, the quasi-ethos of unstoppable

desire embedded in a décor all pink slashes and glass top. There were those
we had to see die naked in hi-res, but also dim as distant stars. Sheryls
and Savannahs déja-vued. We are so familiar with their murders, their
swan songs

seem lullaby extracted from the fine-grained elegance of thrift, the riddled
logic of low-budget in locations that aped affluence but peeled. Pre-heroine
mystique and shabby chic on Home and Garden: everything a project.

All we wanted were Jacuzzis and fake tits in standard, simulated manses,
false fronts easily restored to boomtown grandeur, pumpkins blinked to
limousines,
and sex to strike investigators dumb with violations: senselessness, a theme.

Sheryl died, but was reborn in our extremities as twitch, behind closed doors.
There would be sequels, reckonings, returns. The past came back to
underscore
and settle claims when it could feel a market through the scrambled screen

of quelled impulse and shame, knew itself classic: cool, crisp and cheap
to remaster, product of a world long since gone silver, silver bangle and bright
pink, the yellow kitchens painted over, shag torn out for parquet floors—

polished black and white squares bursting with scheffleras and house
palms in granite pots beneath cathedral ceilings. Nude, blonde Playmates
floating dead in heated, indoor pools. Tastefully shot, hauntingly scored.

We knew cathedral ceilings— knew the ins and outs of hanging art, knew
hallways and the gleam of walnut banisters foretelling accidents,
things coming to a head: the mother's smile, the antique cuckoo clock,

the owl's moving eyes. Tic-toc of the suburbs, synched, and calling down
an orchestrated storm of nightmares not to be believed. Rather, to be
known, but dismissed glibly for the loft of many mirrors. To be sure,

the final, frosted reds of welcome mats endured beyond all reason
on the sagging, weathered stoops of broken homes. After the explosion:
smoke, an old hit single. Sweetie, things went platinum. And we soared.

Night in the Old House

The muffled voices of late night comedians permeate
the countryside, called into our homes by parabolic dishes:
coastal drive all hoary ear and silvered palm, meekly cupped
in prayer and faithfully responded to, till zap! Uninterrupted
signals proof of special favour, guys known, buddies in low places
with your back. Derivative design, as comfort, beats dead air,

evicts unpleasant thought. Alas. Sallow figure-eights present
around the eyes, reflecting grief's pathologies, holistic circuits
all centered in the gut, the epiglottis, little studied glands.
The brain, whichever part, a panicked nurse, attempts a slew
of fragmented novenas. Nervous mothers linger close,
humming a lullaby that breaks after the chorus, and resumes,
breaks and resumes, until I can't distinguish grace, or god,
or self, from old, canned laughter deriding the day to come.

What We Believe

The human eye casts no light of its own.
What we see in the dark begins within:
a vulning pelican in the swan's breast,
a scarab beetle foregrounding the moon.

Cameo, intaglio: deep-set crests and hares
in battered maria. When the doorbell rings
at 3 a.m., I see my body slit from abdomen
to clavicle, a crouching lynx emerging from

tree limbs lanced to the walls in sodium arcs,
coming one step closer, every car. A half-
remembered rumor, that ex-con: hacking his way
surely from news clippings and lead stories

into the locked house, switchblade stashed
in shirtsleeve and the horror movie glare
of broken window shard in red right hand.
I believe this. In that split: my decorative

teapot hurls itself onto the tiles, tempest free
and wild as a bat, bright blood in the owl eyes
of my pine floors. If there is a man, shivering
on my porch, rubbing his hands, he'll see me look.

See me see him huddled in the bluster of high winds,
mid-March and minus ten. No vehicle in sight.
A silhouetted woman come alone to tend the bell,
no one around, and nothing to substantiate a pit bull.

If You Are Receiving This

You will get your wish tonight. Found love
will enter your fever as ice chip, slid beneath
the tongue. Solace will envelop the lamina,
pierce the radix and fill you with light. Soothed
to your core, you will tumble after, fetch the pail
and buy the cow, the magic bean too, cakewalk
through your sacraments under pleasant scrutiny,
nurse fat newborns in the downtown core,

like living's easy. Somebody you know will die
of mesothelioma, grandfathered in on the fibrous
mineral: first known address, summer lover, liquored
slip-up come to dig its claws into your latest happy news.
Unsubscribed, a lurker wants to monitor your sugar.
Have you ever cried for someone? Does that person
know you? What if you could kiss this person? Dno't
eb sprusired fi oyu acn raed tihs. Here is a list of fishy

miracles. Ask me: It is 1:51 a.m. I don't ever drink
any pop, well maybe ginger-ale if yer sick. Coffee???
Tequila. Red summer waitress. This is getting way
too serious. Green apples. Single. Lexus, Shadow,
just that one time ;) in the graveyard, over thirty, self-
employed, witch. I will never, never tell you. Boxers,
kisses, eyes and asses. I would have to say my breasts.
My kitten. Christmas. Seven. Not that I know. Maybe.

Never. Maybe. Guess. *Everybody* checks the time stamp.
What is really on your mind? Maybe you should call
your sisters, they will tell you to live every day. They
will remind you: reason, season. Truly works, now make
your wish. This could happen to your daughter. This is what
the man will attempt. Normally, I wouldn't do this, but
only the heartless remain unconvinced. Somebody wishes
they could meet you. Whisper your password to them.

Assumption Rock

I mean, we found this perch, but co-factors abound,
traumatic nicks reorienting saplings we'd predicted

would lean right. Predators, invaders, arrogance:
something interferes, intercalates, leaves us with an order

we can't map, deep current sequelae skewing surface paths
from points of origin we couldn't dream up if we huffed

the contrails of the highest climbers in the history of comers
so provoked by the night sky they'd stake their lives on flickers

and not flinch. Which leaves us heaven's bowl, conviction,
GPS. Seats us at the cracked clay shoes of specialists

with everything to lose, doggedly translating comets, spheres,
into careers and Divine Right, amygdalae still forcing every hand.

The Rural Lynx

Little is known about our rural lynx cats.
Few remain, and they remain occult.
If they prowl into town it is over
sheets of hard-packed snow that will not snap
when padded on. So, they come silently:
broad, silvered paws leaving no prints.
Adept, they cede no tufts of fur to our
chain-link fences. No surveillance cameras
catch them on forays. Bound, and with
them bound the fortunes of leporids,
to a blinking, ten-year cycle, sister to the sun's,
of calm and storm, grasses and dearths,
boom and bust — to the vegetable wheel —
they adhere, and biding, barely trouble us.

Hard Cores

Nobody likes to make concessions.
We cannot share space, nor walk
through walls. What of ourselves
we lose or launch into another's fold
cannot be relied on to send word,
even if it marries, or it plunders
and survives. Even when familiar
voices bring us news of how we fare,
there is no way to gauge sincerity.

Desperate to be let in, eaten once in,
missionary cells work to convert
a muddy sea of lumpen, willful whales
to make one more, or two of one,
or one two without end, but wieldy,
no less. Thus, living as we do,
huddled in thick cloud, lonely and exposed
in lightning season, dialoguing
always trips the bells. I already have a god,

says one. Our aliens make war,
our lovers duel in drifts of nucleated snow,
where live particulates are drilling out
and down, emerging from cold stars
like fighter pilots staggering from wrecks
on sizzling tarmacs— unrecoverable.

The Eye

It used to be with a cigarette,
mad bee to a poison clover,
I would go alone to reflect
on whatever, behind the fence,

and exhale upsets. Now it is
all consequence, real fear
and healthy living. I have
to live with my misgivings,

cope in the evening, kids
in bed, with one glass of stout,
or, more often, cup of tea,
dropping, doubt by doubt,

into the lightest sleep.
So much is mine to keep,
so much mine to prize,
I try to fabricate zénitude

amid the drums and whys
of the den, wiping spills
away. Full heart, blasted mind,
ever the storm's still eye.

SHEDIAC, NEW BRUNSWICK

Hostess

You want to see a live lobster, its cold
stippled chitin, a real bagatelle. I will get one
from the tank to show your sticky kids.

One cringes throughout, suppresses
a lime-face. I have learned to hide
distaste when instructing delight:

now feel for the palp and note the eye.
There is no need to caterwaul. I know
you're tired and it's been a long day

in the backseat, strapped, I totally get it.
Everyone here is on vacation except for *moi*
pi mes collègues. We say *collègues*,

but we are earning our tuition, single
moms banking our hours, a couple teachers,
every other summer a rebellious divorcée,

or owner's wife making a point,
or owner's daughter, plank-walked
into the midden as lesson.

Bienvenue

Lit with floodlights, lobsters dance the *rigodon*
above the stylized traps of glassy booths:
undead, convivial, blood red, monocled.

Shall we give *les touts p'tits* filthy crayons?
Several menus worth of puzzles so you
can consider, at your leisure, what might
be palatable to small, unhardened
animals? They won't like the bisque.

I think grilled cheese, a chicken snack,
sodium and protein with a clown-face,
tailored to their needs—a sensible
concession. I am told you've come to see
the dancers, and you love the violins.

This too is traditional dancing. Feel how
cold the surface of this hard skin, slick
as a rain boot hauled from the dykelands.

Ice

Tinkle and hiss of a shattered mussel shell.
Tempting crackle of mid-spring ice
at the curb. How it longs to be crushed, toed,
broken for the bluntness of its crick,
to have its voice heard. But it's bread

you've come to crack-a-lack in this
beleaguered port, and our ice is astute
enough to swirl itself into exotic drinks
and masquerade as luxury on decks

flanking a patchwork pave adorned
with potted annuals, generic purple
trumpets, snaps, impatiens: heavy,
gaudy flags belying shallow roots.

Flora

It is much too late for lilacs. Look for
lupins and devil's paintbrush or ditch
daisies splayed in loose constellations,
crawling with ants. These familiar petals,
too, inspire a compliance that presents
as charming stoop and mild delusion.

We could all be cured with herbs
and visualizations, eight hours of real,
uninterrupted sleep taken at night.
The day-sleep of our shift workers
is one proximate cause of general decline,
illiteracy in any tongue, defeatism, low
birth rate, mood disorders, single moms.

Many of whom you will meet at the door,
and recognize much later, at the wharf,
hair mussed, sitting on worn bar stools
looking wiped and terribly approachable
in pink, ironic, long tanks plotted to keep
stretch marks under wraps when arms flail
to a pop beat, or a club-mix *rigodon*,
if it is Tuesday night. They've all gone
home with our brothers and exes, bras
billowing out from our fathers' exhaust pipes.

Once, we inked hearts on our hips to outdo them,
took up smoking in droves, tried to quit,
spit our Trident into their ashtrays,
out on the porch while they broke
themselves in on our futures.

Music

God, I so apologize. You're the tourist:
this week is the festival and the fairgrounds
are already packed. You should be on line
for boiled corn and kettle chips, letting
the world be stripped of context, spinning
right round like a record, right round, upside
down bolted into the Zipper, at the tip,
tip, top of the ferris wheel, rocking
nervously in your precarious seat.
And oh my god remember this? The power
ballad rising up is undiluted memory,
is particle and bitch, is sucker-punch
and wave to those below: their cameras,
your nausea, regret and homesickness.
That what it is? It's muffled by the pitchy twang
of folk hits other cities have outgrown.
The cult of *rigodon*: a dizzy cult, a pipe dream
full of holes stoned carnies might crawl
into and corrode. Thus cradles fall
and damaged nerve deceives the heart,
omits the most important detail: cradles fall.
It just forgot just let the violet strobe ripple
your arm up in the swing and sway of fist,
and hit the tent for cock rock cum bluegrass,
things never land up easy, do they Jack?
but take me down the dunes, a divot in the rocks,
my straw flips gone, such short-lived summer
animals tear through us, sing us songs.

Culture

Tonight, the giant helium balloons,
crabs and clamshells in gaudy aluminum,
rustle over the Co-op, and droop like
tranquillized fifties mutants around
the flaking eaves of the liquor store.

The village disperses, deliquesces,
drifts along drooling into the bay,
its drive folded into the fuchsia orange
fever dream of sunset in late August:
the wrong kind of nostalgia for your needs.

The varnished apples, stars and cedar
chips, and the sea shell pomanders strung
with tulle are still available for cheap
in other latitudes, in sunny coastal towns
on other coasts, in every study of the land,

its men and money, its dark hearts carved
after a dark purpose and displayed. This too
is a display, a dark heart proffering sunlight
while I count saleable blessings, quietly:
quahog, apple tree, pin cherry, star. So

much depends on the annual car show.
Please come back again: niche pageants,
the illusion of young girls able to dance,
bowl-a-thons endorsed by local legends,
local legends numbering in the tens.

How do you become a local legend
if you're only visible to tourists
and small dogs? Subsistence is long, long.
It is the ferry home from visiting
your mom. She too is stippled chitin,

knit scarf full of thought and hours put in
to teach you store-bought patterns guarantee
delight. She is the forest green of live crustacean
pearled into reflection you might gift
a daughter with, though pastels are the norm.

Exports

A face emerges. Cross-stitch, herringbone,
pointillist root: freckle on the earlobe
just like yours, the only way to tell you
from your twin. Twin sickness, triplet,
octuplet, semblable. You resemble
every Elizabeth, every Annick
who has ever gone north, hounded
by wolves, lured by isolation pay, adapted
to the cold, and comfortable with distance,
dry towns, loneliness, acres of ice. Anything
to save your mom's house. Nestled there,
part of the church, bank, tree, Shopper's
Drug Mart horizon. Dark ridge of hills
like the blade of a key: her chimney
the last slender tooth in your spare.

Local

You were not supposed to stay so long
considering this waitress, prick bartender
on her mind, absently rubbing her kinked
wrists, absently pricing copper anklets,
cow cream and preservative-free balm
for dishpan hands. She too, is a hawk-
eyed dream snare, webbed willow hoop
the lynx's eye directing hares in that part
of the spirit where aspirations pool,
their surface a blue skin reflecting
clouds and gulls against their will.

Part of her still wishes, but cannot afford.

She's survived the death of possibility
and carried on, preoccupied with other,
closer deaths. The trail of breadcrumbs out:
moldy Rorschachs left by tits renouncing
carbs in the forest full of names and trunks
chopped for the revelation of the rings
inside the stunted eloquence of long,
cold, rooted years observing the upended.

Heritage

Roots like pythons bulge under
thorned loam, squeezing tender, red-
ringed trunks until they pitch, their sharp

tips spearing layered polypores: local
mushrooms we have recognized as trove,
complete with dying language. Plainly,

we collect ourselves. We wring a rare tisane
from our unfortunate reversals, and
cause eglantine to grow, and edelweiss

among the potshards and refuse. It, too,
merits a notebook, industry, kind words—
though cures run rampant through

the unhinged sky in soothing rainbow tones,
dispelling sense. Our hearts have broken,
radically, into crackled tiles, a wide

assortment, scarlartine and grey,
increasingly the norm in summer homes
with floating floors, going up for sale.

And real four-chambered hearts in these
imaginary homes. Overwintering
mechanics wide awake with the cosmology

of roses, looking for remotes. You are
only blotch and crooked finger, guest,
a translation request: *quinze cents par mot.*

Souvenir

The problem of translation: excellent
food, terrible service, boutique tastes
outlasting all—the spinning wheel,
the pewter cod, the cider-press, and the cider
adding value to the whole, affable history,
resolved, repeated. Salty. It, too, is a live
lobster, hoping to be prized, returned
to its display tank. We can't follow

such descents—passages into the lower
reaches of the murk behind clouded glass.
We're sorry you've been made to wait.
We're very busy. We're very busy.
We cannot imagine what is special
about you, or what manner of thing
you have endured. But we have read
your predecessors—what they liked,

the warmth they engendered, the way
an evening can slow the heart, create
a quiet in which to kiss, blissful
among the ice wines on a screened-in
wraparound. You've paid enough
to be enraptured. In this way, we live
for—through—you. Surely
you must see yourselves in us,

our bustle, our exasperation, such
bewitching, educated hungers
to attend, such circles, such
gliding gulls, so much traffic in all
this heat and everything at hand,
on hand, tonight. This too, is almost
worth remembering, exactly.
I can take the picture for you.

CROSSWALK

Stay Away

I'm digging here.
You find other shores.

I want to be arrested

when our picks
clink in the core.

Walk

The sub-basin,
              an ess curve,
gadus-green, sluice of lime,
clastic sed at the bottom of things.

Footprints, petals, what
carboniferous hollow
could predict our hearts,
tongue-tied microflorals,
wanting to, but not. Talk

to me about sunken forests,
about crossing the iced strait
to see if anything.

Mention fossil and rot,
and the bridges
we've got, but stop
in the places
you have always stopped,

              sink mid-word.

This feeble groove.
This hallowed spot
leads me to think
we cannot

have arisen, thin new limbs
up into light, sand
and coralline wrought,
five-toed, mired, starved.

There is a tendency to drop
I have identified.

I know we fought,
but I always believed
we would return to one another easily,
tides yielding to our wants.

Instead, this slow, embittering stalk,
to end as studies, if discovered in the redbeds
among slivered shells and pots.
To have it said: they went upright.
It has become impractical,
embarrassing to walk.

Rotary at Wheeler Boulevard

Moncton, New Brunswick

The tousle of bare trees due East
is a dark, stiff ruff, effigy-still.

The Hub is gristle, grease and rust. It runs
on fumes, held tongues, poker and habit.
Mumbling river's blistered gums cannot recite
the forest any more than we could still incite

the double-takes and accidents we caused once,
dovetailing gorgeously down to the beach.
Filthy winter and the banks are parched,

cracked as our chapped elbows, lips: tolerable
blots. If there was splendor, whatever, it's lost.
My eyes run over listing crosses spiked down
the escarpment, mud-spattered and pecked.

Waiting for Hekate

Awful that it was, and sick with a nostalgia
for the future born of too much early luck,
comes the chiasmus, years stuck
in the hourglass's neck, a car stalled
on the tracks with you inside, confused
but braced for a collision, goddess
of the crossroads not responding to your calls.

Then comes a man, god in his palms,
a haloed salesman, incandescent, backlit
by the near-death haze they continue to sell
in dim auditoriums, one night only,
town to town. Compassion of a promise
in the tranquil laying on of hands,
lunulas effulgent, lustrous nail beds.
Beach snail pink with hope.

The x inhabits you, he says, and not the other
way around. Our lives are swaths
of desert with infrequent conurbations,
conurbations full of deserts, barren plains.
In desert fields, love is the fish
who swims through scorching sand
to bring the flood. And what the flood
disgorges, what resumes—celestial music.

Many voices fashioned your sedan,
do you agree? Let me take you back into
the filigree of ancestors who ferried you along.
This car you sit in is a vesica piscis,
a fish bladder bisecting four-way tracks,
four-way tracks bisecting lemniscates forced
in upon themselves when single structures failed.

Do you understand where two fields meet,
a third is born? I think you should step out
of the car, ma'am. Let me read your palms.
Yes, let me see. What we find in starry furrows
will unfix you, set you free. The way out
the loophole is to put the car in neutral, let it roll.
I will be your pace car. Just follow me home.

Business Class

Flight from Toronto to Boston in June

My need for silver eye liner begins over the suburbs of Toronto
when the bright blue clustered eyes of backyard swimming pools,
the cold, sclerotic stare of prosperous neighbourhoods reminds me

I can easily pretend. How quickly everything becomes a shopping list,
a task, a store to hit. Just now it is the sight of hazel ponds cooling
in old-growth—the city past—all frosted with a rime of algae green,

their antique mint, pastille, expertly lashed. *Quelle belle caprice*, the fields
eye shadow quads, aventurine and auburn, flawlessly defined, ruler
straight lines isolating pastures. Multi-tonal mineral palettes

compress and crack over the border, where a deep smudge
contours meshed agglomeration, drainage wrinkles spooling
from a fine grey vein of river. Getting closer, I believe my yesterdays

in jade can be recaptured with a cunning purchase, under the right
signs, at bargain prices: club kid's lid, the pine and lime of bio-fuel
in Boston. Gutted quarries going startup: subtle greens. My lips are

chapping, and the catalog of wants expands, each item a kinked nerve,
distracting as a sainted summer crush, moved onto Boulder,
ad exec, or something, maven of the mountains, last I heard.

Customs

We take each other in by drawing each other out.
The motley rags yoked up our sleeves are bundled near
the heart: so much to give. A limp-wristed handshake.
Bloodless disembowelments, snip, eviscerations. We drip

intimations in pitch perfect voices. We need a lot from
one another, but nothing extra. No flourish in the signature,
no exclamation marks. Tongues coated white with all the times
of day, we spit each other out like sour pips. We can't

even help our friends. Not like this. Nobody can risk
unwanted growth in time of shift. Or loss of sleep.
Or heart-sickness. We're all going to different places,
and you don't accept gifts in line at Customs. You can't

accept gifts, period, or process claims under these conditions.
Trust does not make economic sense. Even courtesy
provokes us, makes us wry. Cotton-mouthed, we drain
our Nalgene thermoses—bisphenol savvy, cyanide wise.

Take It

When the gut says take it,
it's from feeling you've become
a branded scrap of wrapper
caught on wrought iron,
dead tree or phone pole.

A very specific, discarded thing
that will only incur disapproval.
No one's climbing up to get you down.

The body tires, but remains material,
its relevance intractable. It has to have
its way. So you give it the pill
it needs to go on.

There's a broken record,
juddering in its rut,
stuttering its genius
into no demand.

Parrsboro, Nova Scotia

In the rocky sand under the cliffs, we bit our lips,
and shoulders burnt, knelt to hack white quartz from calcite brick
in geometric shards. All afternoon the promontory
rumbled, flung loose rocks in clouds of silt as if to taunt—

or scare— us out of wanting explanations, or conversing,
teasing insight out of one another's brimming anecdotes.
It was the grimmest summer I had ever known: *go to hell* shot
magic bullet through the Voodoo Lounge, I ruined my own dress

with day-glo rum. Let go of it. We found a slippery cache
of smoky zebra quartz, and fell to sift the sand for lightweight rocks.
There was ugly gravel veiling bluish veins of amethyst. We couldn't
even feel how badly we'd been burnt, skin peeling off, shedding

cells and glitter dust into the weld pool of the flats: rutilating gems.
Eventually, I thought, our colours will streak shells and pattern
carapace with clotted amber, peridots, our stubborn lusts etched
into the ridged lips of univalves, staining the dullest of agates.

Crosswalk

It's not a busy city. Our sidewalks are capacious, we've got room.
You could go a lifetime without bumping heads. Without

being required to circumvent. There are no hidden triangles, no isometric gaffes.
Nothing is oblique, here. Nothing is acute. I saw you on Main Street,

and I turned. Whatever happened to revolving doors? Our banks
are vulgar, they just squat there, vestibular vultures, slotted, rounding corners.

Your face was not expressionless. I thought I saw a question
form and deliquesce, like: if we loitered on a sinkhole would we plummet

to the burrows that connect us, underground, or could we dangle
from the girders long enough to be discovered, snarled in cobwebs,

as it were? The way is open, much too open. What's happened
to porticoes, and what's become of fire escapes? In 1906,

this city burned. And it was swamp, once. I saw you on Main Street
and I turned, abandoned a trajectory I thought was absolute.

On Mingling

After William Meredith

I do what's in character, I look for places
to interrupt you in your small talk
with a well-timed witty remark, or I look
for a place to sit down somewhere
with a book, or I find a plant to consider
and fuss the dry leaves from. I love
to do this, in any case. So it's honest,
and it is so rare that I find any need
to interrupt, and more rarely still, that I should
start a conversation we couldn't finish
given the small time, and the smallness
of our relation. Apertures are increasingly rare,
you know, although—it isn't so much
that they're expensive. It's where

could they go? You don't see screen doors
the way you used to, all the time. We want
sliding doors to all our balconies.
French doors. Double doors into
all the businesses. And maybe double doors
have led to the demise of chivalry—somebody
said that, once, to me, after the strangest
tussle in a vestibule. And I thought yes!
but have they bred a better reciprocity?
We did not agree, but married. Marriage
cannot be the fear? Its specter why
we are the way we are in the crowded rooms
we have bothered to enter, heads on
straight, and feeling hopeful? Screens

at the windows, see, but windows—
anyway, not what I really meant by
apertures. I was thinking more of the voids
we sometimes seem on hand to fill
so squarely it smacks of the fictive.
Too often, I stand on the outer edge
of a close-knit circle doing its philosophy
in self-correcting circles, like it does.
And, though I would like to trigger
a spiral, I stop, mid-wave, to scratch
my head, in case they don't wave back,
and I stand on looking... intrigued
or askance: how else could you?

Slips

A butterfly in Fredericton
starts to text your husband
and the roadside goes gut pink

with livid blooms: keen orchids,
boldly veined, conspicuous
as histories, exposed. You pull

over on the Sawdust Road for slips,
gob-smacked by the angle of the slope.
Years of practiced gesture, dovetailing

defeats. Who knew how much
you'd fail to see, discordant tones
azured with travel guides. You

wanted to ingest the sight of beach
glass and bleached clam shells were
enough to stimulate a dopamine

cascade. The lucent green of tide pools
cooling between slopes persuaded
you to trust. Any qualms erosion

stirred seemed an appropriate response
to the trifling tingle of ghost crab
hatchlings scuttling over your toes.

Four O'clock

In other news, my love, the car has started
making a sound. It has all the qualities of song.
A ticked crescendo keeps time with the crawl
of government and bank traffic, predicts a little
accident. The afternoon coagulates, dribbles

a circumference of poles. Overhead, a wedge of geese
glides south, their shadows slim kayaks on bleached cement.
No idling in the jam for them: their past is sloughed by
movements practiced as a player's sidelong glance.

At home, garlic from China sprouts green blades.
We can't bring ourselves to eat it: origins too remote.
Our roots are as, or more far-flung, for all we know.
Still, we go at each other like wolves.

Accident 1

Mailbox dimpled, a plundered hut.
Belly slit: entrails sliding red and blue
in big sale letters down a slope of snow.
Sun hitting everything hard. Balance

owing: $26,789 intact, the fact of it
wedded to ice-cloaked rock.

Envelope soaked and shredded, through,
shreds pulled into a stiffening star.

Accident 2

I was doing someone a favour,
when, by drift, the day bookended
in a crooked neighbourhood. Please,
it will only take you ten minutes. Please,
there is nobody else I can ask.

Salt had eaten away the lines,
and why imagine the lane might cease
all at once, with a buried logic,
all at once contiguous to
the lie of the true main road?

On the horizon, headless maidens
linked their arms with quarterback
and quarterback, lowing electrical
giants, monstrously disproportionate.
Banded, they cast a dreadful net.

I watched their shadows battle
and engulf the slender trunks
of birch trees on the lovely hillock
I was coming to. And huffing, climbed
out of my spun and tilted car,

and staggered like another lost Pleiad
into a square of sun, winnowing as
the war raged on, as curlicue and filigree
locked horns with thick, black strands
slung low between bristling nests.

Accident 2, cont'd

The officer was adamant.
This was not an accident, ma'am.
I almost thought he would prattle of fate
or claim that we were meant to meet
in dim, shuttered January, on this icy peak,
as elemental forces drawn into a dance
whose motions all reshape the world.

Bat of the lash, to sidestep the fine,
but oh, I assure you it was. Cruelty
of sun, pitiless salt, and frankly,
horrid design—trickery and neglect.
Your green eyes were an accident, ma'am.
This here, car in the ditch, a mass
of brutalized alder stumps,

we call that a collision, or crash,
and drug or fatigue or inattention
or lack of skill, not accident
was the cause. That's what the report
will say. Judging by the time of day,
type of collision, and affect, ma'am,
I'd wager you're overtired.

Maybe an accident of perception.
That falls under lack of skill.
If anything, I'd say too much attention.
Lack of skill, again, or some drug.
My green eyes were a calculation.
That is not for me to decide.
What if we called it misadventure?

I was cold and hungry, so admitted
to fatigue and took the warning.
He called for a winch and waited
with me. Later, I retraced the waking
dream of perpetuity that led me down
the gulch into a quarrel I couldn't win.
Trust in my instincts, their music, fled.

ACCIDENT 3

Trying to keep true
in sticks of rain:
brittle spines wreck
on the windshield,
break open and let go
the semi-opaque fluids
of their brief integrity
to be dashed, further
dashed and blown off
in the syncopated fervor
of mechanical black blades.

Then cut to the chick,
the girl in the road,
her silver cloak, barreling
Ford, impervious hicks,
the swerve, the flight. The silver
torn, filthy and flapping.
Sapling as stent.

And the wish of the blades,
beating cut—cut to
the dawn fog. Years later,
safely housed, we wake
to crickets, flood with
their harrowing song.

Biological Hazard

Dispose of it, but how? It has suffused
the way-stations, fogged into our synapses,
washed its filthy hand

in every impulse. Magic wand, cadabra:
this is that. That thing we talked about
forgetting, feeding to the wolves and let the devil,

this is that. And virulent. Metastasizing,
tansy in a ditch. Our lime culvert is
insufficient. These are needs

no situation could contain. No liberty could match.
Containment: did I mention there's a bat,
berserking in the bedroom? We are trapped.

Leachate in the sinew. *Try*. Apotheosis, how
would that suit? All abstraction, everything allowed.
You are a snake, you know that? You are

Lucifer, himself. Oh, come again. Say again.
Once more, with a little heart,
and like you mean it, disappear. Be odorless

and colourless, and catch me unawares. I cannot
do this to myself. Your palm prints
on my body, under elms. We missed the boat.

We are lost cargo. We are toast. A lane
of smoldering bonfires threads the coast
in our long wake. Forget me. Choose to forget me

every day. If I seep into your garden,
tell a lie. An oxidizing barrel fallen from the sky.
Who might have known? Who might have guessed,

someday, a family would live here? Find
a junkyard. Lay me down in mufflers, slashed
car doors, expired plates, and when it's finished

boil your clothing. Lock your doors. And hunker down:
            effluvium patrols and contravenes. Be neutralizing,
find groundwater, go there. Say goodnight,

the t of night, a coffin nail, tapped out.
Do you hear sirens? Put a lid on. Put a lid on, tight.
If wishes were horses, kiddo, alchemists would ride.

Leave

Dead willows prefigure some divorces.
If you're headed out, the brittle salix
recommends it, clings to frost and wants
to be transfigured. It envies millers,

the gauzy-winged, prototypes, moist,
unwrinkled casings. And green, coiled
larvae with the patience of spare tires
resigned to sullen modesty, long winters.

Listen: even pliant boughs
are snapping *fuck this* in the chill,
the sobering blast, its killjoy prescience.

Place

Say it is a dovecote,
not a pigeonhole, though
once you've made such claims
there is no going back.

You have held eleven jobs,
and not one management.
You cannot fake that into
a grace. Say it is a dovecote:

place a sheer, violet scarf
over the standard issue desk
lamp. What have you made
beautiful? Violet murks

your deluded nest, accentuates
the clutter. Nobody will love
you here. Say it is a dovecote.
You can see for meters.

Blue Quarter Hour

In morning's geodesic grace, lambent violets twist
from awnings of porphyry, rippling xanthic tarps,
cumuliform in amber, lilac-fringed
—the nerve of elegance.

Relax your eyes and the yard mackles, pales
into a field of loosestrife and wild mints.
Red maple's ripe plum domes double and spread
over liatris crenellating aster settlements,

and in the distance, blue flag's slender purple ribs
convey the fallen sky's crushed hues to petal's edge,
arcing over patient rhizomes nestled in wet cedar.

Luck

You're still a frozen rudiment,
a smidge, a blackened blueprint
leaning as if dead against a corm.

One dewy drop is not enough to prove
there is a spring worth trying for.
Little tendrils up: a tepid mud,

the roar of sap, disembodied legions
angling for the light. The drill again:
forced goodbyes, banal ascents,

the over-eager meeting with disaster.
Song of birds you cannot help but answer:
catalyzed, called out, you see a widening

blade, the retort of an unexpected, early
flower, four-leafed and defiant, rousing
panoplies, the season-long gala of honeyed

exhalations. Stepped on, sucked, sucked up—
could be impossible to brook. Even the plucked
are shrugging seed into the bestial green pool.

Petrichor

The concrete's perfume rises, redolent
and bodied, after rain. Yarrow, ringed
by brook lobelia, vetch, and lady's rocket
merges with musty, weathered fences.

Plum-bruise of the sky holds sodden maple
throbbing from the drenched lawn, green
all slammed-thumb swollen with the countless
broken bodies of the rain that fall and fog
between the heavy sky and pavement.

In the plaza, potentillas and spireas share
their beds with wild roses and echinacea.
Purples eddy curbside, in puddled gasoline
beneath a sidling, silvered lilac — softening
a heritage of steel, of parking lot and tar.

Parched earth and cement exhale the ghosts
of shrubs and saplings. The garden hangs a row
of torn delphiniums, vessels crushed in mist.
We breathe it in like aerosol, slick it on our skin.

True Love

In the car again, scanning for the tower
that broadcasts fate, distant voice
reminding me: it never did run smooth.
Engine trouble, potholes, punctured

tires and dead raccoons, red porcupine
moguls on the shoulder, fusillade
of gravel set in stiff musculature.
Noble antlers. Last apprehension before

the swerve. Worst thing you could do
is slam the brakes on, leaden colossus
trundling behind you. You wanna
go out in a crisis of metal, bleed out

in a bedlam of fractures and char?
Those who make it don't think twice,
careen into startling, last ditch u-turns,
dispersing the gathering murder of crows.

ARRAY

Worm-bodied chaos, lump and tangle, sag
of the grey-painted back decks, chipped stoop

dirt swirling, crag and nook clots, hair and heel
slough, pumice dust, dander caught in carpets

filthy as baleen, threadbare, grey. Gravel,
ground in stains and gunk caught in the city's

many blistered drains and throats. Strewn roses,
sickness, strewn plastics, Kleenex: a thought glides

through you orderly as an Edwardian
physician, polished stainless as his blades.

Sunflower

The seeded amber of your star face
goes misunderstood. Its whorled eye
unlike the lion cubs and tigresses that smile

up from cultivated violets and *pensées,*
beguiling us. You of the slow sip,
the long day's nod, peering over

the picket fence, leaning up against
wrought iron bars like a nice lady
jailed for an aberrant crime,

you are both a comfort and too
beautiful, your symmetry writ
too large. We know the spiral's

golden angle is utilitarian, but hell.
It packs a called for sunny punch.
Even chopped and bundled

on the kitchen table, you're a wallop,
striking us just so bright and unguarded.
You leave us silly with cheer.

Acknowledgements

Thanks to all the magazines in which some of these poems have appeared—*The Fiddlehead, Arc, Prairie Fire, The Malahat Review, CV2, The Dalhousie Review, Room, Riddle Fence* and the now sadly defunct *Dandelion*. In particular, thank you to every single editor who sifted through a slush pile, read my poems, and thought "maybe" or "yes." Without their votes of confidence in my early work. . .well, I don't know. I might have kept a badly maintained blog.

Special thanks to *The Antigonish Review*, who selected "Talk of Mermaids," "On Mingling," "Night in the Old House," and "Bois-Joli" as winners of the 2009 Great Blue Heron Prize.

Thanks to Naomi Lewis and Rona Altrows, the editors of *Shy: An Anthology*, published by the University of Alberta Press, for including the poems "On Mingling" and "Crosswalk."

Thanks also to whoever it was who selected the first line of "Talk of Mermaids" as one of the best first lines of a poem published in 2009 for *The Best American Non-Required Reading 2010*, edited by Dave Eggers. That was cool.

And thanks to the Writer's Federation of New Brunswick, which selected a version of this manuscript as the winner of the 2011 Alfred G. Bailey prize.

Thanks to my friends from UNB's Creative Writing Program, circa 2007-2009, and thanks to Ross Leckie for help early on in the process. Thanks to Stephanie Yorke for always being willing to read and offer feedback.

Thanks to my editor, Clarise Foster, for helping me weed the garden.

Thank you, most of all, to my husband Tyler, for always helping me find time and ways to write. Not an easy task.

About the Author

Jennifer Houle's poems have appeared in numerous literary journals over the past ten years. Her work has won several awards, including The Writer's Federation of New Brunswick's Alfred G. Bailey Prize for best poetry manuscript, award for *The Back Channels*. A lifelong East Coaster, Jennifer grew up in Shediac, New Brunswick and now lives in Hanwell, just outside of Fredericton, with her husband and two sons.

ECO-AUDIT
Printing this book using Rolland Enviro Print 100 instead of virgin-fibre paper saved the following resources:

Trees	Solid Waste	Water	Air Emissions
2	77 kg	6,301 L	253 kg